EXTREME LIFE

MONSTERS OF THE DEEP
DEEP SEA ADAPTATION

BY KELLY REGAN BARNHILL

Consultant:
Robert C. Vrijenhoek, PhD
Senior Scientist
Monterey Bay Aquarium Research Institute
Moss Landing, California

Capstone
press

Mankato, Minnesota

Fact Finders are published by Capstone Press,
151 Good Counsel Drive, P.O. Box 669, Mankato, Minnesota 56002.
www.capstonepress.com

Library of Congress Cataloging-in-Publication Data
Barnhill, Kelly Regan.
　　Monsters of the deep : deep sea adaptation / by Kelly Regan Barnhill.
　　p. cm. — (Fact Finders. Extreme life)
　　Summary: "Describes adaptations that occur in the deep sea environment, including general
adaptations and examples" — Provided by publisher.
　　Includes bibliographical references.
　　ISBN-13: 978-1-4296-1264-7 (hardcover)
　　ISBN-10: 1-4296-1264-9 (hardcover)
　　1. Deep-sea animals — Adaptation — Juvenile literature. I. Title. II. Series.
QL125.5.B37 2008
591.77'9 — dc22　　　　　　　　　　　　　　　　　　　　　　2007020897

Editorial Credits

Jennifer Besel, editor; Alison Thiele, designer; Linda Clavel, photo researcher

Photo Credits

Corbis/Lynda Richardson, 15; Getty Images Inc./Minden Pictures/Norbert Wu, 5; jeffrotman.
com/Jeff Rotman, 21; MBARI 2004, 20; Minden Pictures/Dr. Bruce Robison, 22–23; Minden
Pictures/Norbert Wu, 17; National Oceanic and Atmospheric Administration/Department of
Commerce, 28 (left); Nature Picture Library/David Shale, 13; Nature Picture Library/Doc White,
cover, 24; Nature Picture Library/Jurgen Freund, 26; NOAA, 28 (right); OceanwideImages.com/
Gary Bell, 8–9; Seapics/Dave Forcucci, 11; Seapics/Ofer Ketter, 8; Seapics/Rudie Kuiter, 12;
Shutterstock/Andy Heyward, 27 (notebook); Shutterstock/Gert Johannes Jacobus Vrey, 27 (mask
and snorkel); Shutterstock/Helder Almeida, 6; Visuals Unlimited/HBOI/E. Widder, 7; Woods Hole
Oceanographic Institution, 25; www.norbertwu.com/Norbert Wu, 18–19

1 2 3 4 5 6 13 12 11 10 09 08

TABLE OF CONTENTS

CHAPTER 1 How Deep Is Deep? 4

CHAPTER 2 Adapt or Die 10

CHAPTER 3 What's to Eat? 14

CHAPTER 4 Gulpers and Vampires — Oh My! 18

True Lives of Scientists 28

Glossary 30

Internet Sites 31

Read More 31

Index 32

HOW DEEP IS DEEP?

It's dark. Really dark. And so, so cold. The ground is covered in thick muck. Then it falls away into a trench that seems to go down forever. In the darkness, something moves. A glowing, ghostly creature unhinges its enormous jaws and shows its razor-sharp fangs. It's ready to bite, and it will not miss.

Where are we? Some science fiction movie? Or maybe a nightmare? Nope. This is real. Scientists are only just beginning to understand the scary world of the deep sea.

Most of our planet is covered in water. Two-thirds of it, to be exact. People have only explored and studied 1 percent of the ocean's depths. That's not much. But in that tiny portion, scientists have found amazing monsters lurking in the dark.

anglerfish

OCEAN ZONES

SUNLIGHT ZONE

TWILIGHT ZONE

MIDNIGHT ZONE

Down into the Zones

The world's oceans can be divided into zones. If you have ever played in the ocean, you have been in the sunlight zone. The sunlight zone is the top part of the ocean's water, where people can swim or fish. The sunlight zone is only a tiny part of the ocean. The ocean floor plunges to impossible depths. Imagine sinking the world's tallest mountain into the deepest part of the ocean. Despite its height, the mountain would still be covered by a mile (1.6 kilometers) of water.

cystisoma

predator: an animal that eats other animals for food

Moving down 492 feet (150 meters), you'll enter the twilight zone. This zone doesn't get enough light for plants to grow. Animals have to get good at hunting if they want to eat.

Every animal has to look out for hungry **predators**. Some animals are really good at hiding. The cystisoma, for example, is completely see-through. Even its organs are as clear as glass. What a great way to avoid being seen and eaten!

Going even deeper to 3,200 feet (975 meters), you'll come to the midnight zone. The midnight zone is the most mysterious, least explored, and largest biome on the planet. More people have gone to outer space than have visited the ocean's depths. Why? One word — **pressure**.

Imagine you're lying on the ground and someone puts a full milk jug on your chest. Not so bad. Now imagine that you have 10 jugs on you. Now imagine 100 jugs. You're probably starting to feel a little uncomfortable. Now imagine that the stack is taller than a house or a skyscraper! How do you feel now?

People can only travel deep in the ocean in a deep sea sub. These subs are made to survive the pressure.

box jellyfish

In the midnight zone, the pressure is so strong that it would crush your body. That's because people have **adapted** to the conditions on land. For a long time, scientists thought that the deep ocean was a totally empty place. Imagine how surprised they were to find large groups of strange animals adapted to the harsh conditions of the deep.

CHAPTER 2

ADAPT OR DIE

All creatures adapt to their environment. If they don't, they die. It's that simple. Down at the bottom of the ocean, animals have adapted in some pretty amazing ways.

First, how do fish survive under all that pressure? The bodies of deep sea fish are different from those of fish in the sunlight zone. The fish you're used to seeing have an organ that helps them float called a swim bladder. But a swim bladder is filled with air. It would be crushed under the pressure. Deep sea fish don't have a swim bladder. In fact, their bodies have adapted so they don't have any air pockets that could be crushed.

CRAZY!

The giant squid has the biggest eyes in the world. Each eye is about 12 inches (30 centimeters) across.

lanternfish

Lighting the Way

The bodies of deep sea creatures have adapted in other ways too. It's dark way down in the ocean. Deep sea animals have developed some tricks to help them see in the dark. Some fish have enormous eyes. These large eyes help the fish see what little light there is.

brooch lanternfish

CRAZY!

Scientists think that about
90 percent of deep sea animals
use bioluminescence.

Other fish have taken the light thing way
further. They can make their own light using
bioluminescence. They have chemicals on their
bodies that make them glow in the dark. Animals
use their light to scope out hunting grounds, find
mates, or lure curious fish into becoming dinner.

viperfish

Ferocious Fangs

If you were a deep sea fish, what feature would you want that would help you get food every day? You could choose to have lots of very, very sharp teeth. When food is scarce, every bite counts. Several layers of razor-sharp teeth that hook inward help fish dig in so food doesn't wiggle away.

CHAPTER 3

WHAT'S TO EAT?

Ok, so you're a fish. And not a big one either. You're starving, and there's not a lot to eat down deep in the ocean. What do you do?

You could eat **marine snow**. This material drifts down into the ocean's depths. What floats down? It can be anything from tiny pieces of dust and bacteria to fish poop, feathers, and dead bugs. The remains of dead fish, algae, and plants are part of marine snow too. All of this stuff floats down, like a softly falling buffet. Fish love it!

marine snow: small pieces of plants, animals, and bacteria that clump together and fall to the bottom of the ocean

MARINE SNOWBALLS

INGREDIENTS:
- a bunch of poop pellets
- a dash of bacteria
- two or three planktonic foraminifera (single-celled organisms)
- one diatom (a tiny organism that can use light to make food)
- a splash of dust

STEPS:
1. Let all the ingredients mix together to form a sticky ball.
2. Wait for the ball to float down from the sunlight zone.
3. When the ball gets to you, gobble it up quick before another fish gets it.

INTERVIEW WITH AN ANGLERFISH

INTERVIEWER: Here we are down under the sea. I've just found an anglerfish and I'm trying to get an interview. Ms. Anglerfish!

FISH: Shhh! You're blowing my cover.

INTERVIEWER: So sorry. I was hoping you could answer some questions.

FISH: What do you want to know?

INTERVIEWER: Well, it's awfully dark and quiet around here. How do you find anything to eat?

FISH: See this light on my head? When it glows, fish get curious and come check it out. I swallow them up before they realize what's going on.

INTERVIEWER: You just swallow them up?

FISH: Down here you don't want to miss out on a feast. My stomach stretches to hold big meals, so I don't have to let anything go to waste. Now, if you'll excuse me, I think I see my lunch.

Moving

Another way that some animals get food is through **migration**. More food is available in the upper levels of the ocean. Every night, millions of tons of fish move between the twilight zone and the sunlight zone looking for food. It's a lot of work, but it gets the job done.

anglerfish

migrate: to travel back and forth from one area to another

Watching and Waiting

Other deep sea fish don't waste energy chasing down prey. Instead, they wait for prey to come to them. Many of these fish have expandable stomachs and jaws that unhinge. When prey finally swims nearby, these fish have enough room inside to gulp down a big meal.

CHAPTER 4

GULPERS AND VAMPIRES – OH MY!

They have fangs so long that their teeth don't fit in their mouths. They can smell food hundreds of yards away. They are ferocious. They are clever. And they are hungry. Want one for a pet? Not a chance. Here's a look at some of the animals that make their home in the deep sea.

On second thought, maybe you should skip this chapter. It's too scary for you. If you keep reading, beware of monsters in the dark.

That poor hatchetfish is pretty much viperfish sushi.

CRAZY!

Don't try to swim down to where these deep sea animals live. Your body would be crushed like a pop can.

The vampire squid can see in the dark using tiny lights, or photophores, all over its body. This squid uses the lights to see. It turns the lights off to stalk prey. Its eyes, compared to the rest of its body, are huge. How big? Well, the vampire squid is only 6 inches (15 centimeters) long, but its eyes are the size of a wolf's. All the better to see you with, my dear . . .

The basket starfish looks like a tumbleweed rolling across an open plain. It lives in waters reaching 4,000 feet (1,220 meters) deep in the northern Atlantic Ocean. Unlike other starfish, they don't stop at five small arms. Their arms keep branching out farther and farther away from their body, acting as a kind of net. This adaptation allows them to gather more food than they would otherwise be able to catch. These starfish can reach almost 20 inches (51 centimeters) across. They use their many arms to catch and eat unsuspecting plankton.

One species of anglerfish is extremely committed to fishing. It has its own net and lure attached to its head and chin. It has a glowing bulb that floats above its head. Hanging from its chin is a garden of glowing whiskers, waving in the water like delicious weeds. Imagine the poor fish that sees those lovely, glowing, waving weeds. It swims closer and closer. It's so close it can almost touch this strange garden. Instead of finding food, the unsuspecting fish is greeted by a set of sharp, ferocious fangs. Actually, the victim probably wouldn't even notice the fangs. It would already be food.

An anglerfish can swallow prey that is up to twice its own size. Yum!

CRAZY!

Only female anglerfish have lights and fangs. Males permanently attach themselves to a female, and their only job is to mate.

The gulper eel is not a friendly sea creature! Gulpers can grow up to 6 feet (1.8 meters) long. Over time, the gulpers' jaws have become more flexible and expandable. This adaptation has helped them to become more efficient hunters. They can gulp their victims whole, which is, of course, how they got their name.

hydrothermal vent: a hot spring on the ocean floor

CRAZY!

Water around a hydrothermal vent can reach a temperature of 700 degrees Fahrenheit (371 degrees Celsius).

Along the ridges of the ocean, **hydrothermal vents** spew hot, poisonous water. Nothing could live near these, right? Wrong! Shrimp called *Rimicaris* live quite happily near these vents. These shrimp eat bacteria that live in the mud. They've also developed simple eyes on their tails which help them look for the glow of new vents. Amazing adaptations!

These tube worms have no mouth or gut. Bacteria in their bodies absorb energy from underwater gasses.

Oceans Full of Life

From the icy waters of the ocean's floor to the blazing hot hydrothermal vents, oceans keep surprising scientists. Scientists once thought that the deep oceans were empty. They thought there was no way anything could live down there.

ADAPTATION ADVENTURE

Today you are a deep sea explorer. You're safe in your deep sea vehicle, ready to brave the depths of the ocean. You've got your hands on the controls, your eyes focused on the blackness all around you, and you've just spotted a brand new creature!

What adaptations does this creature have to survive? What does it look like? How does it get food? Draw a picture of the creature and write a paragraph describing its special adaptations and how it survives in the deep, dark ocean.

But as scientists explore the oceans, they find out about the amazing creatures that live deep below the surface. New creatures are being discovered every day, proving that living things can adapt and exist where we least expect it.

TRUE LIVES
OF SCIENTISTS

As marine scientists explore the deep, dark ocean, hydrothermal vents are an area of great interest. The creatures that live near vents can survive one of the harshest environments on planet earth.

Tube worms survive and thrive near the vents.

The Search for New Life

How do scientists get down there? They hitch a ride on Alvin, a deep sea sub. This sub was built to survive the enormous pressure in the deep sea. Three scientists can squeeze into Alvin and dive to almost 3 miles (4,828 meters) below the surface.

On the outside of the sub, there are tools that help scientists collect information. A wand protects a thermometer and tools that measure chemicals. The wand also has a tool called a "sipper" that collects water samples. Moveable arms outside the sub allow scientists to catch creatures and bring them back to the surface. Scientists are always looking for something that has never been seen before.

Eventful Discoveries

Scientists study the bacteria found at these vents to discover how they survive. Some scientists think information about this bacteria will help them find new ways to make food and medicine. Also, they are looking at ways we might use this bacteria to clean up oil spills in the ocean.

GLOSSARY

ADAPT (uh-DAPT) — to change in order to survive; a change in an animal or plant is called an adaptation.

BIOLUMINESCENCE (BUY-oh-loo-men-e-senss) — the production of light by a living organism

BIOME (BUY-ome) — an area with a particular type of climate, and certain plants and animals that live there

HYDROTHERMAL VENT (hi-dro-THUR-muhl VENT) — a hot spring on the ocean floor

MARINE SNOW (muh-REEN SNOH) — pieces of plants, animals, and other materials that fall from the sunlight zone

MIGRATE (MYE-grate) — to travel from one area to another on a regular basis

PLANKTON (PLANGK-tuhn) — tiny animals and plants that float in the ocean

PREDATOR (PRED-uh-tur) — an animal that eats other animals for food

PRESSURE (PRESH-ur) — a force that pushes on something

INTERNET SITES

FactHound offers a safe, fun way to find Internet sites related to this book. All of the sites on FactHound have been researched by our staff.

Here's how:

1. Visit *www.facthound.com*

2. Choose your grade level.

3. Type in this book ID **1429612649** for age-appropriate sites. You may also browse subjects by clicking on letters, or by clicking on pictures and words.

4. Click on the **Fetch It** button.

FactHound will fetch the best sites for you!

READ MORE

McMillan, Beverly, and John N. Musick. *Oceans*. New York: Simon & Schuster Books for Young Readers, 2007.

Pfeffer, Wendy. *Deep Oceans*. Living on the Edge. New York: Benchmark Books, 2003.

Woodward, John. *Midnight Zone*. Exploring the Oceans. Chicago: Heinemann, 2004.

INDEX

anglerfish, 16, 22, 23

basket starfish, 21

cystisomas, 7

deep sea adaptations
    bioluminescence, 12, 20, 22, 23
    expandable stomachs, 17
    lack of air pockets, 10
    large eyes, 10, 11, 20
    large teeth, 4, 13, 18, 22, 23
    unhinged jaws, 4, 17, 24
deep sea subs, 8
    Alvin, 29

giant squids, 10
gulper eels, 24

hydrothermal vents, 25, 26, 28–29

marine snow, 14, 15
migration, 16

ocean depth, 6
ocean zones
    midnight, 8–9
    sunlight, 6, 10, 16
    twilight, 7, 16

predators, 7
pressure, 8–9, 10, 19, 29

Rimicaris, 25

scientists, 4, 9, 12, 26, 27, 28–29

tube worms, 26, 28

vampire squids, 20